KV-523-496

Publish and be damned
www.pabd.com

Canine Behaviour Practice

Angela J Coupar

-

Canine Behaviour Consultant

Publish and be damned
www.pabd.com

© Angela J Coupar

First published in Great Britain 2005 by   Angela J Coupar.
The moral right of   Angela J Coupar to be identified
as the author of this work has been asserted.

Designed in London, Great Britain, by Adlibbed Limited
Printed and bound in the UK, Canada or the US.

ISBN: 1-905277-40-7

Front Cover Picture: William - Border Collie on
Campbell Town Beach in Scotland.

All the dogs pictured throughout this publication are our own dogs that we have rescued or fostered over the years.

*"To those people around
the world that help to make a better
life for the animals we love."*

<u>Authors Note:</u>

I find my work not only interesting, but very rewarding and over time I have met some wonderful people and dogs.

Almost weekly, I get questions on how to set up a behaviour practice. So rather than continually sending out the same replies I decided to write this short book as a basic guide to setting up a small business as a Canine Behaviour Consultant.

This book describes how I established Canine Angels and how I run my own practice. I hope that you find the information not only interesting, but helpful.

Angela J Coupar
Canine Angels - Behaviour Consultant
Certificate in Dog Psychology

Contents

<u>Acknowledgements</u>

To my husband for his continued support, advice
and understanding throughout my canine and animal
ventures, I couldn't have done it without you.

To our own Border Collies, who never cease to amuse us with their
antics and eagerness to learn. To the many rescue dogs and puppies
we have fostered over the years who gave me the inspiration to follow
my dream of working with animals and to the many dogs and other
animals that pass through our door via the Canine Angels Behaviour
Consultancy and Acre Fen Pet Day Care & Home Boarding Services.

With many thanks to everyone who took the time
to proof read my manuscripts, including
Debra Bragg the Director of the Canine Behaviour Centre.

And finally, to all those pet owners, friends, family and
colleagues, including behaviourists, trainers, dog walkers/sitters,
animal healers and vets throughout the world of dogs and animals
who have given me the inspiration to achieve my goal...

"Litter of Border Collie Puppies. Fostering these was a joy."

Introduction:

Several years of experience with owning my own dogs and through fostering many puppies and adult dogs from the charity I supported as a foster carer. To rehabilitating and training the rescues ready for their new homes, but also as a Trustee on the Board of Directors helped to build on my interest to own and run my own small canine related business.

Through the many books I have read and learnt from, including those written about animal behaviour by Dr. Peter Neville, Dr. Larry Lachman and Dr. Stanley Coren to name but a few who ignited my own thoughts and interest about canine behaviour.

Reaching my goal of running my own business as a behaviourist took a lot of hard work and research. These combined with an eagerness to highlight the need for positive training techniques that are not only safe, but far more effective than the old traditional methods of training and rehabilitation to be implemented by those involved with animals and finally, a desire to help the many dog owner's reach a solid and enjoyable relationship with their canine companions.

Border Collies have always interested me as a breed, with their eagerness to learn, ability to work and their ability to live life to the full. Through the years I have been lucky enough to work closely with this breed and learn to understand their natural behaviours, enabling me to adapt and re-channel their energy using mental and physical stimulation.

Sadly, far too many Border Collies along side other working breeds end up in rescue centres or in homes that simply cannot cope with their high energy requirements, or have the necessary understanding to live with such active breeds. With these natural behaviours and the inexperience of the owner, far too many end up with behavioural problems that may have been prevented at an earlier age if they had been trained correctly.

As a behaviourist with knowledge and understanding, it puts you in a position to provide advice and support so that these problems can be modified or eradicated. With this I knew I could make a real difference to the dog owner's and their dogs.

The Canine Behaviour Centre is run by an excellent team of behaviourists and trainers who provided me the opportunity to study my chosen subject and to point me in the right direction for establishing a business. Once I had passed their Dog Psychology course and qualified as an Associate Member I was able to plan my future.

Two courses are available from the Canine Behaviour Centre, and come highly recommended.

- Dog Psychology
- Aggression

These courses provide a thorough understanding of psychological theories and techniques, whilst enabling the student to work through each stage at a pace that suits them. These courses provide the necessary information to learn and gain a competent understanding of subjects ranging from Canine Behaviour Therapy, Development and Social Behaviour, Cognitive Processes to Assessing and Diagnosing the various types of behaviour problems a behaviourist will come across.

For more information on the courses available from the Canine Behaviour Centre and other sources of education, see my resource page at the back of this book. Gaining a qualification in this field should be your highest priority before considering a career as either, a Canine Behaviourist, Dog Psychologist, Therapist or Trainer.

Since establishing my business, I have received many enquiries from students already on relevant courses, to people simply interested to how a person can become a behaviourist and set up their own practice. I am always happy to provide advice, but naturally this can be time consuming with replying to every enquiry with similar advice. This is why I decided to write this short book as a guide to anyone interested in this profession. Finding the right help can be difficult, especially when this is your first business venture and nobody likes to get it wrong as mistakes can cost you money.

This is a basic account on how I established my own business 'Canine Angels' and is intended to provide you with the information required to decide if this is the right career option for you.

After reading this publication and you do decide to venture further into this field of work and set up in business, I hope that the information will provide a valuable guide in pointing you in the right direction.

One important point I do wish to stress, is to be careful on how you describe yourself, as there are subtle differences between an Animal Behaviourist, Dog Psychologist, Canine Therapist and Behaviour Trainer. Get this wrong and you will suffer the consequences. For example, you can only describe yourself as a Dog Psychologist if you are a student in the science of canine psychology, or have qualified as a practitioner in this field and studied the disciplines as those mentioned below for an animal behaviourist. A Dog Psychologist will use approaches such as, Behaviourism, Psychoanalysis and Cognitive Psychology and specialize in canines. Where as an Animal Behaviourist is qualified to assess and treat a wide range of animals and will have a more in depth understanding of several disciplines. These disciplines include Psychology, Biology, Ecology, Genetics and Zoology. So please get it right before you start practicing.

"Sharing - Bracken with puppy Rosie. Puppies need to learn to be sociable with other animals as well as with people".

Considering A Career As A Canine Behaviourist

This is not a career you can just decide to set up as a business because you happen to love dogs and have owned a family pet for a few years. There is more to being a behaviourist than simply providing a little well meaning advice that in some cases may not be the correct approach. A wrong diagnosis and incorrect behavioural advice can create more serious behaviour problems for the dog, risks to the owner, their families and the general public, as well as giving you and your business a bad reputation that may result in legal action.

You will require knowledge and understanding of canine psychology and evolution, cognitive processes, development and social behaviour. You will need to be confident with dogs of all breeds, able to communicate well with people, be able to explain and demonstrate the techniques used in behaviour therapy and just as importantly, have some form of qualification to show you have the ability and understanding to make a diagnosis and provide the necessary advice. You must also be able to construct a detailed report in the form of a written behaviour modification programme for clients.

If you are sure that this is your chosen career, then take a look at the resources at the back of this book for recommended courses. Remember, new theories and training techniques are always being researched, so keep up to date with progress and attend as many conferences as you can to remain in tune with other behaviourists, as well as enhancing your own knowledge and experience. Research is the way forward to understanding our canine companions further and being able to teach them how to behave acceptably in an ever changing environment using positive reinforcement techniques that get results and make learning enjoyable for not only the dog, but for the owner also... You can never stop learning something new in this profession and that is what makes it so important to keep in touch with any up to date research, theories and training techniques.

Once you have the qualifications, understanding and some experience with dogs of different breeds, then you can consider starting up in business. This is not an easy profession to get immediately off the ground and will take time to establish, especially if there are several other behaviourists or psychologists in your area.

Research is also important when considering establishing your own business. You should start by looking into other similar businesses in the area. Find out how much they charge for consultations and if they specialize in any particular area, such as aggression, separation anxiety, or if they combine their behaviourist businesses with another pet service such as dog training, grooming, dog walking, sitting, etc. This will enable you to offer similar services or something unique to yourself at competitive prices. High service fees will certainly not be seen as competitive and your enquiries will be less profitable in the long term.

Consider starting off part time until your client base increases before going full time unless you are confident that you can earn enough to live comfortably. If you do not wish to take this option and go straight into running a full time business, then consider combining your business with, as already mentioned other pet related services. This will also help you gain experience and raise interest from potential clients. For example, working in boarding kennels will help to gain further canine experience with a variety of breeds. Discuss with the kennels, if they would permit you to hand out business cards as a behaviourist, or to place an advertising flier in their office.

Converse with your local vets and other pet services in the area and get them interested in your business venture. Having a vet to refer clients is something I personally recommend. See if you can persuade one of them to let you spend some time in the surgery observing their clients and if possible allow you to provide some behaviour consultations for one afternoon and try to encourage them to increase on this. However, please make sure you are fully insured before providing any behavioural advice. If possible ask a local behaviourist if they will enable you to sit in with them for a day, as this will give you some idea on how to approach a consultation yourself.

Once you have gained a qualification and understanding, the only real way to gain experience is to get out there and have a go! You will have the ability and knowledge, so take your time, be thorough with your assessment and your confidence and experience will develop.

Working with dogs is definitely a rewarding, interesting and enjoyable career, but not always well paid, so don't expect to become a millionaire...

This career also means that you will need to cope with barking dogs and potentially aggressive dogs at close range. You will come across dogs that may inappropriately urinate for whatever reason and you will most certainly get slimed on by a dribbling canine, of which some breeds are worse than others. You will soon learn the body language of a dog just about to shake his head and disperse a spray of saliva and when to move out of the firing range. So it's certainly not a glamorous career.

Although every individual dog and its behaviour is different, you will have days that are repetitive with the type of problem, but naturally not the cause of the behaviour. Just like a vet who spends a good amount of time a week administering annual vaccinations and neutering. You as a behaviourist will also have weeks where you have several dogs with house training problems, or dogs with various forms of separation anxiety. Basically don't expect to have unusual cases filing in through your door every week.

Building up a respectable business takes time, hard work and the ability to specialize. Remember, there is a lot of competition in this profession, with some excellent behaviourists, so be prepared... Until you get established you will have many ups and downs.

"Many dogs can be re-trained not to chase livestock"

<u>Health & Hygiene At Work</u>

If you do decide on your own consultation room, either from your own home or a rented room, then please make sure that you implement good health and hygiene control.

Your working environment should be disinfected regularly. Use a good commercial product. I use a product called TriGene as my disinfectant cleaner. It's not cheap at around £10.00 for a litre, but it does go a long way (Prices subject to change). This product is used by many commercial businesses, such as veterinary practices and boarding kennels and can be used in many ways, including disinfecting floors and work surfaces. Medichem International also sell many other products including the OdoGene products which absorb, neutralize and re-odourize with pleasant fragrances and ideal for any canine accidents. (See resource page for website).

A complete first aid kit is also essential in this profession as you never know when you may require some antiseptic and plasters. I also have a canine first aid kit available. You never know what is around the corner, so it's best to be prepared.

Always have an accident book and keep it up to date. Even the smallest graze should be accounted for in this record. In the case of a claim being made, you then have written information to refer to.

Finally, if providing refreshments for clients, then make sure that all surfaces, crockery, cutlery, etc, are clean. Don't forget to include refreshment products in your monthly expenses.

"Best Of Friends - Elsie & Wilma"

How To Set Up A Practice:

Start off by designing a 'Business Plan' as this will help you to formulate where you are now, where you want to go in the future and how you are going to reach that target.

Your Business Description: This should be a detailed account of what your business definition is:

The Company Name: In other words, how are you going to trade: For example: As a Dog Psychologist, Canine Behaviourist, Behaviour Therapist or Trainer?

You need to decide if you are going to call your business by your own name or use a title, such as Canine Angels. Try and use a letter at the beginning of the alphabet as these will naturally appear near the top of any directory listings.

What Services Are You Providing: Behaviour Consultations, Puppy Advice, Individual Dog Training, etc...

How Are You Going To Provide Your Service (s): Will you see your clients in their own home? Run a consultation room from your own home? Or rent a consultation room? Naturally, seeing the client in their own home is best, but not always possible. Seeing clients in their own home is also naturally more cost effective than rented premises, as these will include costs for rent, lighting, heating, etc, although having your own consultation room within your own home is also a good option, especially for those clients that prefer not to have you visit them. Keep your options open... If you do use this option, then consider installing a second phone line, or a separate ring tone for business calls, so that you can always answer in a professional manner and have a note pad and pen available.

You also need to take into account that seeing clients in their own home increases costs such as travel expenses, which in rural locations can start to mount up. You will see fewer clients in one day because of all the travelling and then if you are female, you will need to consider your own safety as a woman working alone. Client details should be written down clearly in an appointments book, so you can be located. Trust your instincts and if in doubt as to the credibility of the person, take sensible precautions such as contacting them on the number they provide. Incidents are rare, but these days it is advisable to be cautious!

In What Ways Will Your Practice Stand Out From Others: In what way do you differ from other psychologists, behaviourists or trainers in your area? For example: Will you only specialize in dogs, visit clients in their own home or offer other pet services, such as one-to-one dog training, grooming, etc.

Business Research: Understand your market and who else is working in your area. Look in the local directories, and where possible look at their websites and see what services they provide and how much their services cost.

Identify who your clients will be and how they will hear about your services. Research what people in your area are prepared to spend on a particular service that you will be providing. More importantly, identify any niche areas that no other behaviourists or pet businesses are offering. For example, you may wish to specialize in aggression related behaviour, or hold 'clicker' training classes.

Advertising: Some of the best advertising is 'Free', so before you start, get as many free listings in directories, such as Yellow Pages and the BT Phone Book, as these both offer one free line in their business sections. Make sure you include what you offer. For example: Canine Angels – Behaviourist – Address - Tel No:

Many websites also offer free listings, so look into your local sites and search the internet for dog sites that offer a free listing or link to your own website. For fee based advertising, then shop around as many charge per click on your link, or you can pay higher fees for the larger internet providers, but remember that most of these providers ask for an annual fee.

Place advertising fliers and business cards in local shops, Boarding Kennels, Pet Shops, Rescue Centres and veterinary practices, etc, and in built-up areas post leaflets through doors. Shop around for business cards and you will find some excellent prices or even a free selection where you only pay for the P&P (See my resource page). Making your own fliers is a cost effective way of advertising and enables you to highlight the services you offer. With a little time and patience, computer programmes such as 'Microsoft Word' and 'Microsoft Publisher' you can design all your own stationery.

Design a website, as these can bring in business when advertised correctly on the internet. There are several good free website providers on the internet and are great for an initial website as you require no html knowledge as they provide a site builder and all the templates. If you do want a professionally designed website, then these can cost anything from £90.00 upwards (See the Resource page for Stainton Web Design and the host for my own site Canine Angels). Remember, if you have a site professionally designed, then you will most probably have a webmaster who will charge an annual fee. Make sure if choosing this option, that regular updates will be free and that there are no hidden costs. You will also need to pay for your domain name. It usually costs slightly more to have a '.com' than a 'co.uk'. You will also require an email address for any online enquiries.

Build A Pricing Plan: A properly developed pricing plan will ensure that you reach your targets and work at a profit and not at a loss. Avoid initially under pricing your fees. Increasing them later will not be cost effective and well run businesses tend to reduce their fees, rather than increase them. Above all else, you should be competitive and keep your chosen fees for at least 12 months, as introductory offers can appear amateur and in this profession a Spring Sale really does not work...

To develop your 'Pricing Plan', initially start by working out all your costs, both fixed such as lighting, wages, car depreciation and variable costs, such as postage, telephone, petrol, etc. Remember to include costs of stationery, advertising, insurance and telephone/internet. Secondly, you need to work out a forecast cash flow which is a breakdown of the money coming into and going out of your business. To achieve this, I use a computer spreadsheet every month.

Insurance Requirements: Make sure you are covered by insurance. Public Liability and Professional Indemnity is recommended, but you may also need Employees Liability if you employ staff and may also require specialist job related insurance, such as a policy to cover you if you get bitten and are unable to work. (See the Resource page for Insurance Companies).

Solicitors: It is a good idea to have access to a solicitor who will be available to advise you on any legal issues that may arise.

Plan For The Future: Work out how you want your business to develop. For example: Will you need to update your computer with more workable programmes or to improve your business database? Will you require any additional staff, such as a secretary? Do you have plans to expand your business by offering other services like individual puppy/dog training classes? How do you plan to measure your success? Have you a back up plan in case you require financial improvement enabling you to increase your work volume, writing a book or seeking a business partner?

Business Analysis: To enable your business to expand, you will also need to analyse your own Strengths, Weaknesses, Opportunities and Threats now and as predicted in 12 months time.

Business Basics: Understand the basics involved in running a small business. There are several organizations designed to help small businesses, but here are a few guidelines:

Self Employment Details: Consider which will be the most effective way for you to trade? Identify the advantages and disadvantages of trading as a limited company. Understand the legal requirements of VAT, National Insurance and Income Tax. Register with the Inland Revenue online (See resource page). This is easier than trying to do it by telephone and the website has lots of useful information for starting up a small business.

Legal Responsibilities & Regulations: Understand the Data Protection Act and Licence requirements. This is important if you plan to keep client details on file. You also need to understand which Health and Safety at Work practices apply to you.

Business Accounting: Consider the advantages and disadvantages of employing an accountant. Talk to a local free business advisory centre for advice. These can normally be found in most towns and will be able to supply a wealth of information. You need to be able to manage your cash flow and understand invoicing systems and procedures. An accountant could save you a lot of money and time, especially if you have never run a small business before and are not fully conversant with book-keeping, expenses, etc... However, do contact several accountants for an idea on how much they charge.

I would also recommend that you talk to your bank with regards to setting up a separate business account or for a small loan if necessary. Having a separate account enables you to keep better track of your cash flow.

Once registered with the Inland Revenue, they will normally send you out an excellent free manual "Starting Up In Business", which is full of excellent detailed advice and information, which covers all types of businesses. Their manual takes you step by step through the sometimes daunting areas of :

- Record keeping
- Controlling Your Finances

- Self Assessment
- Your business and the Law
- National Insurance
- VAT
- Tax Credits and Allowances
- Where to get further help, and a lot more...

The manual is easy to follow and demonstrates the best way to approach the important points of running your own business.

Terms & Conditions: These are something that all businesses should have. They can include a business definition, general terms, proposals/offers, variations, a basis of your fees, a calculation of your time (hourly or daily rate), any fixed fees, Information on chargeable expenses, invoicing and payment terms, confidentiality, liability, cancellation, law and jurisdiction, etc...

Some businesses even get their clients to sign the terms and conditions as proof that they agree to them. In this case you should keep the signed copy yourself and provide a photo copy for the client.

<u>Training Aids and Booklets</u>

As a behaviourist you will need to have an understanding on how to use the various training aids that are now available, have a number in stock to sell to your clients and be able to provide a demonstration on how to use them correctly during a consultation. My advice is to purchase just a small selection of each, until you get yourself established and make sure that you purchase them at a good price so that you can make a profit from the sale.

The main training aids that I have in stock and use on a frequent basis are as follows:

- **Gentle Leader Head Collars** – two of each of size. These should come with full instructions. However, the behaviourist should demonstrate to the client how to teach the dog to accept the head collar as well as provide the necessary training advice to get the best out of this highly recommended product.
- **Fabric Collars & Leads** – It's amazing how many clients still turn up for a consultation with their dog's straining on choke/check chains. Encouraging the client to opt for a more appropriate collar should always be advised upon. The leads are normally double ended training leads, or standard fabric leads to match the collars.
- **Dog Training Discs** – By John Fisher and includes a training booklet. These saucer shaped discs are used to interrupt unwanted dog behaviour.
- **Clickers** – A small device containing a piece of flexible steel that creates a distinct sound when pressed and released. Clickers can be used in the initial stages of training and provide a clear and precise communication between the owner and their dog.
- **Sound CD** – Used for Desensitizing Noise Phobic dogs who fears sounds such as fireworks, thunder, gunfire, planes and emergency sirens.
- **Taste Deterrent Spray** – Grannicks Bitter Apple. Used as part of the re-learning process to reduce inappropriate chewing of

personal items, furniture, etc. This product can also help to discourage fur biting.

- **Motivational Toys** – These include Kongs, Activity Balls, Cubes and Bones.

I also always have in stock a small selection of affordable booklets, which can be recommended during a consultation. These include:

- **Reinforcement Training For Dogs** By John Fisher
- **Hear, Hear! A Guide to Training a Deaf Puppy** By Barry Eaton

As a behaviourist, you should be in a position to provide any training aids required and be able to explain the importance of there use as part of the re-learning process. Clients will not want to go in search of these items, as most are keen to get started. So be prepared...

Running A Canine Behaviour Practice:

Naturally, every behaviourist has their own rules on how they run their business. So here are some guidelines on how I organize my practice Canine Angels. You will need to adapt these guidelines to how you think they will best work for you. Remember, the practice will be yours, so you should run it in your own way...

When a client has made contact with us requesting help with their dog, we at Canine Angels write down the critical information. This includes the client's name, address, contact number, the breed of dog and the nature of the problem? When this behaviour started and confirm, whether they have tried to correct the problem? It is also important to identify if a vet has health checked the dog.

Behaviour Therapy is then explained. The client is informed that it will only work when implemented correctly and that only positive forms of reinforcement are used. I always make the point that at no time will any techniques involve negative experiences for the dog, but will require time, patience and a lot of hard work on the pet owner's part. Once the client has agreed to the fee, a date is then arranged for the consultation. Canine Angels then forward the client a questionnaire to be completed in readiness for the appointment. The questionnaire I send out simply provides me with some background information that can be filed for future reference..

During the consultation, which should last no less than 50 minutes, and may last up to 90 minutes or more, a clinical evaluation and diagnosis is ascertained. As a behaviourist I always listen to what the client has to say and always avoid giving a lecture. You really do need to be diplomatic in this profession! As a behaviourist you should never condemn any behaviour on the part of the owner, or that of the dog and keep clear of direct criticism.

A behaviourist should have the ability to be flexible with regards to treatment techniques and be in a position to suggest an alternative at the client's request. In this profession you will also need to be compassionate, patient and understanding, as well as thorough with your assessment of the dog. You should allow yourself enough time between consultations as some may extend longer than average. On occasions you will meet an owner who simply feels the need to relieve their own anxieties by discussing more of their pets concerns. Once the problem has been identified and a behaviour modification programme discussed in detail, I then provide a rough prognosis. You really must be honest with your prognosis. For example: If a training technique is going to be time consuming and the end result may not be a 100% improvement, then don't tell the client that the problem is easy to treat... It's unprofessional to offer unrealistic hope and this is why I personally do not recommend that you supply advice over the telephone as the problem cannot be fully assessed in this way...

Once I have all the necessary information, I then summarise the recommended behaviour modification programme in a written report which the client receives by post within a couple of days. A copy should also be forwarded to any referring vet, or if for example, drug therapy is recommended. It is important not to make any guarantees in your letter/report. However, any reservations that you may have as a behaviourist with regards to the safety of the dog's behaviour should be firmly repeated. It should also be noted that the behaviour modification programme should be implemented as recommended by yourself and if progress ceases, the client should make contact with you - the behaviourist for further advice.

As part of my consultation service, I then contact the client for a progress report. This follow up procedure is provided by a telephone call or in some cases a letter normally two weeks after the initial consultation. At this point the client is reminded that I charge no extra for further telephone advice on the assessed problem. This is one area of business that you may wish to alter according to your own business terms and conditions. Finally, any further consultations will depend on the type of behavioural problem being treated and the progress achieved by the owner.

So now you have reached this part of the book, you will have the basic information for establishing a behaviour practice. It is hard work, but worth it...

<u>Seeking Advice:</u>

Since becoming a behaviourist, I have received many requests of email help from people in various countries including the USA and Canada. These people in many cases are glad of any help they can find, but for whatever reason choose not to seek advice locally. They search the internet for information either from free resources or directly from anyone they consider may be able to provide some information.

People who contact you directly don't always expect to pay for the advice supplied. So be prepared to receive these types of questions. It's up to you if you choose to inform them that your services are fee based, or as I have done on several occasions, simply send them some basic information with your recommendations, such as seeking the help of a local behaviourist or veterinary practitioner.

Most people are either seeking behavioural advice or training tips, but there are some people that send in questions that are either on the unusual side or require veterinary attention. One thing these people do deserve is a short reply. It may be time consuming, but it is up to you to be professional. A little advice can go a long way...

When replying to these requests for help, you really do need to be sensible with your replies. For example, If the dog is displaying a form of aggression, then it's best to recommend that they visit a local behaviourist as the chances of getting your expenses paid including flight or other forms of transport to areas other than those local to you just do not happen! You should explain that a local behaviourist should assess the dog in person as this avoids missing any important facts that may be forming part of the behaviour displayed.

Don't think for one minute that you have all the answers from what a person has supplied in a short email. Making a correct diagnosis comes from making an in depth assessment of the dog, owner and their environment. A part from this, your insurance may not cover you for providing advice outside of the UK.

I am not veterinary qualified. Therefore I am not insured to answer health questions. In these cases recommending that they get their pet health checked by a veterinary practitioner should be your response.

However, in some cases you can give some general advice to point the client in the right direction. Here are a selection of some of the more unusual questions I get asked that do not require behavioural advice or training tips.

Location: Nashville, TN, USA
Question: *My dog has a cedar doghouse in the backyard. It is on cement blocks that are on the ground (grass, weeds and dirt). Inside the doghouse is a fur and fabric covered dog bed. Tiny ants have decided that the floor of the doghouse under the bed is the best place to store their eggs. There are mountains and mountains of ant eggs. What can I do to keep the ants out of the dog house that won't hurt my doggie?*

Answer: Firstly, you need to remove all your dog's bedding and give it a good wash in hot water. Then remove the ants and all their eggs from inside your dog's kennel. The safest way to eliminate the ants is by using boiling water which will instantly kill the ants and destroy the eggs. When you are sure that all have been destroyed give the dog kennel a good sweep out , wash with a suitable disinfectant that is safe for animals and allow to dry.

If the area is prone to ants where the dog kennel is housed, then move the kennel to another location in the garden. This should be raised off the ground and the area kept weed/grass free to deter the ants.

Unfortunately, chemicals to kill ants and their eggs tend not to be suitable for use around pets. However, you may be able to locate a product on the market that is safe for dogs once the product is dry. As I am from the UK, you will need to research possible products that are available to you in the USA. Always read the label and for safety keep your pets indoors whilst you treat the affected areas.

Location: Sand Fork, WV, USA
Question: *I have a one year old Boston Terrier. Two days ago he was bitten by something. We cleaned the area on the neck and gave him egg, milk and burnt toast. His eyes are matted and he has weak back legs, and is shaky. Can you advise?*

Answer: I presume WV is West Virginia. You live in a country that has a number of poisonous snakes, spiders and biting insects that can create various reactions ranging from mild to serious. Please do not take a chance with this - see your veterinary practitioner. This bite may require a medical antidote of which your dog may require several treatments before an improvement is recognised. You have done well to keep the area clean, and please continue to do this until you can get your dog health checked. Your dog's matted eyes, weak hind legs combined with the shaking may be an indication that your dog is reacting to whatever may have bitten him. It would help your vet if you can try and identify what may have caused the bite. However, do not worry if you are unsure, as your vet will investigate this further.

"I'm still puzzled as to the egg, milk and burnt toast. Perhaps this is one of those native American antidotes, but certainly not one that I would recommend above veterinary treatment."

Location: Canada
Question: *My dog got sprayed by a skunk twice. I cannot get rid of the smell on her head. I tried tomato juice, several skunk products and baking soda, peroxide. Nothing, seems to work.*

Answer: We don't have wild skunks in the UK. However, here are a couple of tips that are worth a try to get rid of that delightful odour. Whatever product you use, keep it out of your dog's eyes, nose, mouth and ear's. Soak your dog in a solution of white vinegar or lemon juice in water. Leave for a few minutes then rinse well and allow too dry. If this doesn't help, then try this product.

Envirolife Odour Eliminator. This product is 100% natural and safe and is available in the USA and Canada. Apparently, this commercial product is very good for removing those pungent Skunk Odours.

Behaviour Advice:

Some people simply want a quick answer to their question and to simply be pointed in the right direction, so that they can understand their pets that bit more.

Location: UK
Question: *My Boxer puppy Eve uses over boisterous play?*

Answer: Any games that the owner and dog play require rules and sensible boundaries to avoid over excitement and unwanted behaviour being learned as a consequence. By setting boundaries, having consistent rules and implementing obedience training will help too calm your boisterous pup. I recommend that you join a local dog training club and also start daily basic obedience training. Reward all none boisterous behaviour so that your puppy associates the correct behaviour with the reward. By having a lead attached to your puppy will also enable you to correct her as and when necessary.

Location: UK
Question: *I have two x-breed pups from different litters. When we take them on walks to the local park, both are eating anything that they find. e.g. rabbit droppings, grass, sweets, etc. Is there anything I can do to stop this?*

Answer: Some breeds of dog tend to scavenge more than others. Puppies will also naturally sample everything in sight. This in itself can be a risk, which may result in veterinary care being required. You need to be one step ahead of them and as soon as they go to take anything off the floor create a distraction. As soon as they stop what they are doing praise and reward with something positive such as a tasty treat so that they learn to associate the correct act with the positive experience.

Teaching the basic commands and other important commands such as drop or leave will help modify this problem. Praise and reward all acceptable behaviour. Make sure that your pups are fed on a well balanced diet so that they get the correct nutritional intake. You will also find training them much easier when separated, as this will enable the pups to bond individually with you.

Location: UK
Question: *We were given a German Shepherd bitch puppy who is 9 weeks old. I love her to bits, but she has just started being naughty by chewing my furniture. What do can I do?*

Answer: Firstly, this is a young puppy, so be patient and consistent and she will soon learn what is right and wrong. She is not chewing because she is "naughty", as this is a natural behaviour for any puppy, but one you need to channel correctly by providing suitable chew toys, such as puppy kongs, nylabones, high quality rubber toys, soft fleecy toys that are dog-safe, rawhide chews, etc. You need to encourage her to chew on the correct items and praise/reward her when she behaves acceptably. When she chews something she shouldn't simply distract her with something more interesting, then praise/reward her for responding correctly. Puppies learn by positive association (praise/reward), time, patience and consistency.

You can also discourage chewing of your own personal items, door frames, walls, furniture, etc, by using safe sprays such as 'Bitter Apple' and then gently guide your dog to the "correct" item and praise her. Do not punish or frighten your puppy over this chewing behaviour. If you do, then the learning will not take place successfully. An indoor kennel/crate will prevent her chewing anything she shouldn't in your absence, or if you are unable to supervise her one hundred percent. However, these should not be used as punishment, but to aid with the learning process.

"Basic Obedience Training should be encouraged."

Final Word of Advice:

Dogs have retained many of their natural behaviours despite domestication, but they do not train themselves to live acceptably alongside humans and other animals, or within an ever changing environment. Therefore it is up to the owner to guide and influence their dog's behaviour using positive techniques that encourage learning to take place. If the owner is not prepared to put in the hard work, then their dog will not respond as they would hope them too.

It's up to the behaviourist to provide advice on how the owner and their dog can develop a good bond and relationship by following every stage of the recommended behaviour modification techniques supplied.

Understanding, patience, socializing and training provide the key to living in harmony with our canine companions...

"Fun & Games - Bracken with Border Collie pup Bruce"

"Too own a Border Collie, is too own a working, intelligent masterpiece that requires endless amounts of mental and physical stimulation..."

Angela. J. Coupar

Resources:

Organizations & Courses:

Canine Behaviour Centre - List of Associate Behaviourists. Dog Psychology & Aggression Courses.
Website: www.caninebehaviour.co.uk

Centre Of Applied Pet Ethology (COAPE) - List of Associate Behaviourists and various animal related courses.
Website: www.coape.co.uk

Animal Care College - Many animal related courses at various levels.
Website: www.animalcarecollege.co.uk

Association of Pet Behaviour Counsellors (APBC) - List of Associate Behaviourists.
Website: www.apbc.org.uk

Association of Pet Dog Trainers (APDT) - List of UK dog trainers.
Website: www.apdtuk.f9.co.uk

Helpful Websites:

Canine Angels – Behaviourist, Information, Forum, Canine Related Links.
Website: www.canine-angels.co.uk

Arthritis In Pets - Resource site containing information and links on pet health.
Website: www.freewebs.com/arthritisinpets

Dog Breed Information. This is an excellent resource that also includes a list of breeders and rescues.
Website: www.dogbreedinfo.com

Helpful Business Links:

Inland Revenue - Register new businesses online, information, etc.
Website: www.inlandrevenue.gov.uk

Medichem International - TriGene & OdoGene Hygiene Products.
Website: www.medichem.co.uk

Stainton.net Computer Services. Cost-effective web solutions
Website: www.stainton.net

Freewebs.com - Free & Professional web hosting, with website
builder and templates.   Website: www.freewebs.com

Vista Print - Stationery & Premium or Free (not inc p&p) Business
cards.
Website: www.vistaprint.co.uk

Cliverton Ltd (trading name of Lycetts) - For Behaviourist Insurance,
including Public Liability, Professional Indemnity, etc.
Website: www.cliverton.co.uk

SMG Professional Risks - For Behaviourist Insurance, including Public
Liability, Professional Indemnity, etc.
Tel: 0113 294 4000

Neat Ideas Office Supplies - From paper to printer ink cartridges.
Website: www.neat-ideas.com

Viking Direct Office Supplies - Huge range of essential office supplies
including office furniture.
Website: www.viking-direct.co.uk

My Favourite Animal Charities:

Border Collie Trust (GB) - Providing a safe haven for unwanted Collies and BC cross breeds until new homes can be found.
Website: www.bordercollietrustgb.org.uk

Guide Dogs for the Blind - Providing canine support for those who are visually impaired.
Website: www.guidedogs.org.uk

Wetnose Campaign - Fundraising for animal welfare organizations in the UK and abroad.
Website: www.wetnose-campaign.com

Recommended Books:

Here are just a few of my personal favourites:

Dogs On The Couch: Behaviour Therapy for Training and Caring for your dog.
By Dr Larry Lachman & Frank Mickadeit
Overlook Press

Do Dogs Need Shrinks? What to do When Man's Best Friend Misbehaves...
By Dr Peter Neville
Sidgwick & Jackson

Dogs: A New Understanding of Canine Origin, Behaviour and Evolution.
By Raymond Coppinger & Lorna Coppinger
Crosskeys Select Books

How Dogs Think: Understanding the Canine Mind.
By Dr. Stanley Coren
Free Press

On Talking Terms with Dogs: Calming Signals.
By Turid Rugaas
Lagacy By Mail Inc

Positive Reinforcement: Training Dogs in the Real World.
By Brenda Aloff
TFH Publications

Think Dog! An owner's guide to canine psychology.
By John Fisher
Trafalgar Square Publishing

The Dog Who Would Be King: Tales and Surprising Lessons from a Pet Psychologist.
By John C Wright, Ph.D with Judi Wright Lashnits
Rodale Press

Dominance: Fact or Fiction.
By Barry Eaton
(Available from Amazon.co.uk)

<u>Write Your Own Business Ideas Here:</u>